Overcoming Stage Fright

Discover How to Get Over Stage Fright in 5 Easy Steps

by Adonis Lambert

Table of Contents

Introduction 1

Step 1: Improving Personal Conviction 7

Step 2: Practicing "Vision-Based" Confidence 15

Step 3: Transforming Anxiety into a Performance Enhancer 21

Step 4: Playing the Role of the Confident Person 25

Step 5: Becoming an Opportunity Seeker 33

Conclusion 37

Introduction

There's only one beautiful thing about stage fright — it's something that can be overcome by practically anyone. But first, let's face the fact that it's perfectly normal to feel some apprehension and anxiety before speaking in front of a crowd or giving a public performance of any kind. The real problem is that, for certain individuals, this anxiety is nothing short of crippling. They freeze up completely. They become disorganized mentally. Their faces become bright red, their knees knock, and they start to sweat. Simply put, panic ensues.

If you're one of these people who suffer from profound bouts of stage fright, the consequences can be costly. You may pass up on an opportunity for a lead role in a play, or an opportunity to speak at a conference that would help elevate your career. Others may find themselves unable to complete a project for school or college, because it involves speaking in front of a group or classroom.

You're here, reading this now, because you recognize that you have this problem, and you don't want it to hold you back any longer. And I'm here, writing this now, because I know I can help you.

So how exactly can a person shift from teeth-chattering and knee-knocking to feeling absolutely fluid and relaxed? Well, for starters, stage fright sufferers must find a way to disarm their fears and rewire their expectations. That's right, I'm going to help you rewire yourself. If you read and follow the 5 steps laid out in this book, you'll be able to find and apply that crystal calm within yourself that will grant you confidence and poise, anytime you need it. So whether you have an upcoming public speaking engagement you're preparing for, or you want to try out for the local theater's production or Romeo and Juliet – the process is all the same. What are we waiting for? Let's get started!

© Copyright 2015 by Miafn LLC - All rights reserved.

This document is geared towards providing reliable information in regards to the topic and issue covered. The publication is sold with the idea that the publisher is not required to render accounting, officially permitted, or otherwise, qualified services. If advice is necessary, legal or professional, a practiced individual in the profession should be ordered.

- From a Declaration of Principles which was accepted and approved equally by a Committee of the American Bar Association and a Committee of Publishers and Associations.

In no way is it legal to reproduce, duplicate, or transmit any part of this document in either electronic means or in printed format. Recording of this publication is strictly prohibited and any storage of this document is not allowed unless with written permission from the publisher. All rights reserved.

The information provided herein is stated to be truthful and consistent, in that any liability, in terms of inattention or otherwise, by any usage or abuse of any policies, processes, or directions contained within is solely and completely the responsibility of the recipient reader. Under no circumstances will any legal responsibility or blame be held against the publisher for any reparation, damages, or monetary loss due to the information herein, either directly or indirectly.

Respective authors own all copyrights not held by the publisher.

The information herein is offered for informational purposes solely, and is universal as so. The presentation of the information is without contract or any type of guarantee assurance.

The trademarks that are used are without any consent, and the publication of the trademark is without permission or backing by the trademark owner. All trademarks and brands within this book are for clarifying purposes only and are the owned by the owners themselves, not affiliated with this document.

Step 1: Improving Personal Conviction

Confidence begins at home. By home, we don't just mean practicing your performance at home in front of a mirror (though that's important too). The "home" you need to focus on first, if you want to conquer your fear of the public eye, is the fundamental home of your physical and mental wellbeing—your body and mind.

To overcome any significant fears, you'll need to endure some significant mental and physical stress. Preparing well for these demands will play a huge role in your transition from timid wannabe-wallflower to room-commanding fountain of charisma.

Here's the nice thing about step 1—physical and mental preparations can be undertaken in the privacy of your own home. No matter how bad and seemingly undefeatable your stage fright is, the first step to eradicating it won't involve any bright lights or gaping eyes.

Pursuing an optimal state of wellbeing requires the maintenance of both body and mind. Start with your diet, which affects profoundly both your mental and physical faculties. Caffeine intake must be limited. You're jittery enough as is, and caffeine is only going to make it worse come performance time. Other stimulants—unless they're being used properly as prescribed by your physician—are a definite no no too. You want the body to be relaxed, not jumpy. Regular stretches and breathing exercises are a good way to start developing that psycho-physical relaxation impulse. That's right, you're going to need to practice being calm. It's definitely a good time to take up yoga if you've been considering it. Otherwise, try doing a series of stretches each morning and before you go to bed.

Meditation can also produce enormous benefit by helping you appreciate and experience the fullness of every passing moment. One of the problems associated with stage fright is the tendency for the mind to twist and contort itself due to excessive concern for the future. Meditation can help you learn to center your mind.

Meanwhile, there's no substitute for a healthy diet and a regular exercise regimen. A desire to overcome stage fright is thus a fantastic motivation for getting back into shape. As you close in on your performance date, if you've taken good care of yourself and practiced various relaxation techniques, such as stretching and meditation, you should be feeling quite a bit better, maybe even more confident.

Here are some other tips for getting your body and mind into optimal performing condition:

Eat a Banana an Hour Before You Perform/Speak

You've got that hollow, dreadful feeling in the pit of your stomach. A banana can provide some much needed comfort without making you feel too full. Think of it as a kind of performance comfort food.

*Laugh Your A** Off*

Laughter is good for your body. It relieves tension and stress. On the day of your performance, watch or listen to something that makes you laugh. Getting in some good chuckles before show time will not only make you feel better physically, but will also lighten your mood and make you less stiff going into your performance or speech.

Arrive Early at the Performance Venue

The best workers in show business cultivate a habit of arriving early and leaving late. They spend as much time as possible in the venue. They make it their home, a place that is not foreign, but where they feel comfortable and in control.

Talk to Members of the Audience before the Show

If you get the chance, chat-up some of the early show-goers. It doesn't hurt to build a little rapport, but most importantly, a meet-and-greet will break down some of those intimidating notions that you've been using to terrorize yourself. You'll experience the audience as a collection of normal, individual people rather than this mysterious and perhaps terrifying sea of explosive humanity.

Move Your Body

Both before and during the performance—move around some! Whether you're a seasoned pro or the type that trembles with stage fright, bodily movement will help you discharge nervous energy. As an added benefit, if you integrate bodily movement into your performance, you'll do a better job of retaining the attention of your audience. No one wants to watch someone drone on from behind a reading stand. Find reasons to move, walk, stretch, and dance.

Chew Gum

No, don't do this *during* your speech or performance, but while you're warming up, definitely. Chewing gum will discharge some of the tension in your jaw, which is a good thing, especially if you're going to be doing a lot speaking. As a caveat, eat your banana first, and then chew your gum. Chewing gum on an empty stomach may upset your digestive system.

Hum it up

To keep your voice warmed up, try humming through a few different tunes.

Develop Personal Performance Traditions

Call them PPTs if you've got a thing for acronyms. But create them and use them. Some actors never wash their socks, some pray to their patron saints, or put a lucky charm in their pocket, or rub the nose of a bronze statue, or eat a plate full of steamed Jonah crab claws for breakfast on the morning of every show. There's nothing wrong with being a little superstitious, but in all likelihood there's *real value* to crafting a show-time routine that makes you feel more comfortable and prepared. You got this!

As a friendly note, if you do eat crab claws or any other shell fish, make sure it's fresh and properly prepared. Performance day is not a good time for food poisoning.

Step 2: Practicing "Vision-Based" Confidence

Believing in yourself is easier said than done. It would be nice if a light bulb went off every time someone told you to "just believe in yourself," and you suddenly turn into a brand new person brimming with self-confidence. It doesn't work that way. Nonetheless, people keep saying it: "just believe in yourself and your anxieties and fears will go away." And they're absolutely right. Trusting in your own abilities can make fears manageable. But it's important to understand that gaining self-confidence isn't something that magically happens overnight. In step 2 you'll find some practical, actionable ways to improve your confidence level.

"Vision-based" confidence is the practice of gradually breaking down and letting go of your existing vision of yourself as a nervous, meek, and ineffective speaker or performer. If you want to cure your stage fright, you'll need to replace that vision with a new vision for yourself. A new version of you who is dynamic, interesting, and is an engaging performer.

Hard work in the form of expert preparation is the first step to swapping out the first vision for the confident second one. Preparing your butt off for your speech or performance, thoroughly researching the role or subject matter, method acting (experiencing your everyday life as the character you're playing), practicing your speaking parts; all of these preparations can be undertaken regardless of how terrified you are of what's going to happen when the lights go up. Forget about that for now, just prepare. Just work. And keep working until you can look in the mirror, all worn out, and say to yourself, "I've done all I could do to get ready for this performance. Win, Lose, or Draw, if it's meant to be it will happen." And boom—there goes all the pressure. It's (so) much better to fail or fall short after giving it your all. If you've given all you have to give, then you'll never need to wonder what might have happened had you tried a little harder.

So, if preparation is inversely proportionate to taking down performance pressure, how does one maximize preparation? Here are a few ideas:

Start Early

Especially if you're worried about stage fright, get busy preparing as soon as possible. As you practice, begin to cultivate a vision for what your ideal performance will look and feel like and follow that vision. Every night before you go to bed, settle yourself into sleep by reconnecting with that vision. When you wake up in the morning, connect with it again. Think about your great performance as much as possible.

Know Your Lines

One of the most common fears of performers or speech makers is that they're going to forget their lines. While you can't cure this fear in one fell swoop, you can take every possible measure to ensure you know your lines backwards and forward. Practice is a good start. Practice in front of the mirror, your family and friends. If there's no one around, set up some empty chairs and practice in front of them. Come show time, if you've put in your practice time, your brain will want to cooperate. Even if you're nervous you'll find your lines flowing out from you almost subconsciously. This early auto-pilot is often enough to help you find your confidence and follow through with a deft and inspired performance. Practice is the enemy of stage fright.

Keep Feeding the Vision

If you find your ideal performance vision getting stale, add to it. Imagine the audience giving you a standing ovation. Imagine positive reviews or commentary in the newspapers. Play out a scene in your mind where your fellow cast members and your director are congratulating you on a stellar job. Imagine greeting your friends and family members after the performance and knowing they are honest when they congratulate you on a fine performance. Imagine flowers being flung to the stage, and see if you can't drum up that feeling you know you'd get when taking a bow after giving an amazing performance. Remember, whether you give a great or horrible performance, the sun will still come up the next day. You're not visualizing success because you're afraid of failure. You're visualizing success, because you expect to be successful. If you find yourself drifting into a negative daydream, that's perfectly normal. Make a willful effort to counter every negative vision with three positive ones.

Put It on Record

Another way to gain more familiarity and comfort with the idea of giving a speech or performance is to record it on audio or video. You'll be able to watch or listen to it to review your performance, but more importantly, you'll start to become more comfortable with the reality that you're going to be *giving* something over to the scrutiny of the public. They'll ultimately do what they want with it, love it or hate it, and you must prepare to accept that. Recording your speech or performance will help reinforce that this dramatic artifact is something that's yours to give.

This will hopefully develop in you a sense of purpose and intent. Performers are 100 times more convincing when they believe that no one else in the world could ever play their role or give their speech as well as they could.

If listening to or watching yourself gives you the heeby jeebies, don't fret. It's normal. Many seasoned performers still can't stand to see themselves on video, even after hundreds of performances. But if you can manage to stomach it, reviewing your own recorded performance can help you smooth out the glitches and rough spots. Listen carefully to your tone. Watch your body language. What can you add or cut out that will make your performance more compelling? If you can get to a point where you can watch your recorded performance and see that you've really dialed it in well, then you'll have every right to be mega-confident as you approach your live date.

Step 3: Transforming Anxiety into a Performance Enhancer

It happens so many times. A performer hustles and works hard, giving everything they have in preparing for a performance. But when the time comes to perform in front of a live audience, they still feel unprepared. This story actually has a very happy ending. Their performance is great! All that anxiety and stress and worry somehow gets repackaged, and they deliver the performance of a lifetime, 100 times better than anything they accomplished during rehearsal or during a recorded session.

Learning to feed off one's anxiety is a powerful tool for performers. Some performers get really worried only when they *don't* feel anxious, i.e. if they get too comfortable. That's when they know they've either gotten cocky or lazy.

So, if anxiety can actually feed a performance, then people who have severe stage fright have it made in the shade, right? Not exactly, but they aren't far off. Rather than hunting the stomach butterflies down to extinction, all they need to do is tone down their fear to a point where it's healthy, not debilitating.

The first step in reducing your anxiety level to an acceptable one is to pay attention to and think about how you're feeling. If you really do suffer from stage fright, then your fear of performance is leading your mind to a very dark place, where you feel inadequate and alone. If your anxiety is at a controllable (or productive) level then you will feel a mix of excitement with your fear and a satisfying sense of challenge and opportunity, an overall psychologically healthy feeling. Recognize the dark, gloomy feelings as ultimately irrational; no one's going to die if you don't nail your performance. The stakes probably aren't as high as you think, but you still feel this persistent dread. There are likely some other emotions underlying this feeling that you should consider. Do you generally feel yourself a person of little value or little talent? Are you attempting to relive an emotionally devastating episode from the past? Inspect and come to terms (as best you can) with any psycho-emotional vulnerabilities that may be needlessly inflating your fears.

As you practice your routine of positivity, striving to counter your fears with "Vision-Based" confidence, take action when you find yourself feeling a particularly dark or hopeless emotion. Go for a bike ride, or out for a walk if it's a nice day. Spend some time doing a hobby you enjoy. Engaging in fun, positive activities can help you free yourself from nasty pockets of negative energy and help you tap into more healthy states of being. Remember, you don't have to cure your stage fright at this point. Anxiety or nervousness is fine, but don't tolerate despair.

Another way to cultivate a healthy, empowering self-image is to get away from yourself entirely. Not by escaping into a TV Show, but by doing something constructive for someone (or something) else. Volunteer at the local animal shelter, or go visit someone in an assisted care home. You'll quickly discover how wrong you were about having nothing valuable to offer the world.

The more you can convert nervous despair into nervous excitement, the better you'll do on performance day!

Step 4: Playing the Role of the Confident Person

Even if you're not acting, you've still got a role to play. One of the things that absolutely kills the satisfaction and credibility of most any performance is when the performer brings up the fact that he is nervous. You're on stage. If you're nervous, people will be able to tell for themselves. You don't need to remind them. Audiences hate when performers draw attention to their own anxiety, because it takes them out of the show. We go to watch performing arts because we want to be entertained or enlightened in some way. We're not there to gawk at someone's vulnerabilities. Drawing attention to your anxiety during a performance only makes the audience feel that same type of discomfort, along with an unpleasant compulsion to try and "be nice," and patient with the performer. The audience is there to see a show, not to babysit.

This may sound a little harsh—and if for some reason you do let it slip out that you're nervous, by all means don't continue to beat yourself up over it; just move on—but understand that your role as a performer or speaker is to come across as worthy of occupying the time and attention of your audience. You must always *play the role* of the confident person, even if you don't feel confident. The audience needs you to do that for them.

And you've got the wind at your back. The second you set foot on stage, the audience automatically believes you're a confident person. Otherwise you'd never have taken the stage in the first place. Run with this. Believe you're there for a reason—you are—and give the people what they want.

You can't have good stage presence without good body language. When you practice, work on maintaining a good, straight, upright posture. Practice projecting your voice in a way that will be both normal sounding and audible at long range. Look straight ahead at various focal points in the audience during your performance. Don't slouch and don't ever look down at the floor unless it is called for in the script. When you maintain sound posture and speak with confidence at an adequate volume, you should start to *feel* a lot more confident and at home on the stage, even if your knees were knocking hard from the beginning.

With all these tips and tricks to masterly stage presence bouncing around in your mind, it's important that you be natural and at ease, not constantly going through a mental checklist of things you should be doing properly. You don't have to be perfect and silky smooth with every movement and utterance. If you're performing in a play then your goal is to come across as human, and humans don't always have perfect posture or perfect cadence in their voices.

If you're giving a speech, then yes, you should be as eloquent and persuasive as possible, but you should also allow yourself room to be approachable. Make a joke or two, especially if the subject matter is really dry, as you'll most likely need to do this to keep the audience's attention. If you stutter, or misspeak, so what! Forget it and move on. No one's monitoring you with a notepad making tick-marks every time your speaking is found to be less than impeccable. Remember to smile and to laugh. The audience wants to believe that you're perfectly comfortable up there. Let them.

Whether you are pretending to be Joan of Arc for a play, or just a competent public speaker giving a speech about nuclear power, *act* in a convincing manner. Bury yourself in your "character," and try to think the way your character would think. If you spend enough time immersed in the complexities of whom you're trying to portray, then you will begin to lose sight of your personal worries and anxieties. Some actors even go so far as to stay in character for days or weeks at a time. While this isn't the standard route to overcoming stage fright, it's not necessarily an ineffective one.

Content is important. From an actor's standpoint, certain plays appeal to certain audiences, and knowing that your audience is going to be responsive to the content you're presenting can help put the performer(s) at ease. The same can be said for speeches. Audience reactions will vary. If you're giving a speech on a dry topic, do all you can to make sure you are able to engage the audience. Add some stories to your presentation, even if they already relate to your topic in a positive sense. Stories can be used to draw impactful analogies. Sometimes it may even be better for you to pull out an anecdote seemingly out of left field, so long as you can ultimately tie it in thematically to your main topic. As mentioned previously, humor can also be used to spice up otherwise dry content. You want to get the audience on your side and quick. Comedians, for instance, will tell you that when they're bombing (failing to get laughs) on stage, they can feel the downward momentum build when bombing begins to feel inevitable. Believe me, it's not at all fun knowing that you've got to slug your way through another 15 or 20 minutes with a hostile audience on your hands.

Another way to sharpen up your content is to spend some time thinking about and planning your time frame. Be sure to wear a watch during your speech, so you can at least loosely monitor your pacing plan. How long do you want to spend discussing each point in your speech? Where are you likely to lose the attention of your audience, and how can you polish up these weak points? If you can't polish them up, then shorten them. Mark areas in your speech where you will want to pause in order to give the audience a chance to think, digest, or laugh. If the audience doesn't end up responding in the way you anticipated, don't miss a beat. Pick right back up and move on. A good example of maintaining rhythm when audience reactions don't go as planned can be found in the monologues of late night television. When Jimmy Fallon's joke misses the mark, he usually won't acknowledge the lackluster audience response but instead quickly moves on to the next joke. Occasionally, comedians like Fallon, will self-deprecate some after a botched joke attempt, but if they do, they do it with speed and confidence, betraying no sign of personal dismay.

One common mistake that actors and speechmakers commit when they suffer from stage fright is talking too fast. They feel the sooner they sprint through their lines or their speech, the sooner they'll be done with this most uncomfortable experience. Or, they may feel that their content is uninteresting and that they will burden their audience less if they hurry through it. The truth is that if you talk too fast the audience is not going to appreciate it, but will more likely resent the fact that they're being made to sit for a speech that even the speaker feels is not worth their time. Slow down. If the material is complicated and boring, maybe go even a bit slower so you can give the audience time to think and take from the content the elements that are relevant to them. Being able to share a few silent pauses with your audience is the mark of a good speaker. Slowing down some will also make it easier for you to enunciate and project your voice at an appropriate volume level.

You've no doubt seen your share of speeches. You know what a comfortable, confident speaker looks like. Even if you don't see yourself as a person with a talent for public speaking, if fear is holding you back, start by just *acting* as if you were a person comfortable speaking in front of an audience. *Play this role* as best as you can and as much as you can, and you will inevitably realize at some point that it's not as hard as you first made it out to be.

Step 5: Becoming an Opportunity Seeker

The final step of overcoming your stage fright is to become an opportunity seeker. This means, rather than being a person who does everything she can to avoid having to speak in public, do the opposite. If there's an open invitation for prayer, take it, raise your hand and lead a family or church prayer. If you're attending a lecture or public gathering, and there's a call for questions at the end, then try and come up with a question just so you can stand up and ask it in front of everyone.

If you're serious about becoming a good public speaker or actor, then you need to seek out honest feedback. After you give a speech or performance, have someone hand out survey cards so they can appraise your performance. Talk to friends or family members who were in the audience and willing to offer an objective opinion. Have them give it to you straight. If you didn't do that great this time, who cares! You're an opportunity seeker now and you'll have another chance to shine.

While you're collecting feedback, why not seek out a solid mentor, someone who's an accomplished performer or public speaker who can provide some coaching for you? You may not end up with a famous performer as your mentor (though don't rule it out), but even a friend who is like a fish in water on stage may be willing to take you under her wing and give you some pointers. Another place to find a seasoned performer could be your local improv comedy club.

Practicing improv comedy is a great way in and of itself to sharpen your public speaking and performance skills. In fact, being able to make a sudden change of plans during a play, speech or other performance, can dramatically improve your overall effectiveness. Improv is thus a great skill to have for any public speaker, and probably especially so for those who suffer from severe stage fright. Getting used to unexpected twists and turns during a performance will help reaffirm for you that nothing's ever 100% perfect. The key is to carry forward confidently with a smile on your face and adapt as you go. You may have planned everything down to the minute, and that's fine, even good. However, as the famous General Patton once said, "Plans are useless, but planning is indispensable." Have faith that things will be ok no matter what, and take things as they come. If you suffer from severe stage fright, this may sound like a leap into the dark unknown (and it is, sort of), but by becoming an opportunity seeker, you'll soon learn how to always land on your feet.

Conclusion

You're not alone. And you may be surprised and glad to know that you're already in the company of some of the greatest performers ever to grace a stage or speak behind a podium. Stage fright is a normal phenomenon, one that's best managed through practice and persistence.

Here are some last minute tips:

- Remember, the audience isn't holding your script. If you mess up, no one's going to know unless you tell them;

- If you're uncomfortable making eye contact with audience members, try focusing on an inanimate object, like a vase or a tile of carpet. No one will know that you're talking to the furniture;

- Don't eat too much before taking the stage. Digesting food takes a lot of energy and though you don't want to be buzzing with caffeine, you don't want to be sleepy either;

- Unless you're wearing a specific costume, wear something that you feel good in. The better you look, the more comfortable you'll be while in public view;

- Know your cues! One of the most difficult things for singers and actors is knowing exactly when to come in. We tend to hesitate out of fear of embarrassment if we come in when we're not supposed to. But missing our cue to come in can be just as embarrassing for us and for the entire production.

As you can see from the first to the last step covered in this guide, you have to perform at some point in order to overcome stage fright. There's no way for any speaker, whether it's you, your grandma, or the President of the United States to take the stage without any risk of making a mistake or looking foolish. You have to be willing to jump in. This guide, if you follow it, will maximize your chances of pulling off an excellent performance.

Finally, I'd like to thank you for purchasing this book! If you enjoyed it or found it helpful, I'd greatly appreciate it if you'd take a moment to leave a review on Amazon. Thank you!

Printed in Great Britain
by Amazon